THE CUT THE CRAP! GUIDE TO

MUSIC TECHNOLOGY

Artemis | EDITIONS

First published in 2003 by

Artemis | EDITIONS

an imprint of Artemis Music Limited
Pinewood Studios
Pinewood Road
Iver Heath
Buckinghamshire
SL0 0NH

Order No. ART00009
ISBN: 1-904411-07-X
ISMN: M 57025 007 3

Project editor: James Sleigh
Jacket design and layout: Fresh Lemon
Illustrations: Berni Georges
Printed in the UK by Unwin Brothers Limited

www.artemismusic.com

THE CUT THE CRAP! GUIDE TO

MUSIC TECHNOLOGY

ABOUT THE AUTHOR

Gary Marshall has played gigs ranging from Glasgow Barrowlands and T in the Park to five-year-olds' birthday parties, teenage beauty competitions and gangsters' private functions.

He has been heckled, bottled, threatened with knives, harassed by the police, mocked in national newspapers, molested, electrocuted, ripped off, chased by hormone-crazed girls and even set on fire – although not all on the same night.

When Gary isn't running for his life, he covers music, technology and pop culture for a wide range of magazines, newspapers, radio stations and websites. He sings in Glasgow band Kasino, whose website is at www.kasino.co.uk.

CONTENTS

INTRODUCTION: THE TECHNO FILES

"Any sufficiently advanced technology is indistinguishable from magic."
– Arthur C Clarke, *Technology and the Future*

Without technology, the world of music would be very different. Instead of playing drums, you'd have to bang rocks together – and in a world without keyboards or electric guitars, musicians would be blowing into weasels and twanging badgers.

Technology is at the heart of music. Without electric guitars and amplification, there would be no rock music; without keyboards and drum machines, no dance music or hip-hop. And today's technology is even more impressive: it can turn even the most tuneless dirge into a chart hit, and in the right hands it enables you to create music that previous generations could only dream about.

KEEPING IT REAL

In the 70s, the Musicians' Union campaigned against keyboards because it felt that such infernal devices would put 'proper' musicians out of business. Today the union welcomes high-tech musicians, but the 'keep it real' brigade hasn't disappeared. People who believe that music isn't music unless everyone involved has a beard have popped up to complain about almost everything: sampling, dance music, computers and most recently, AutoTune.

AutoTune is a computer program that fixes tone-deaf bellowing, and it's used extensively on records by B-list celebrities. But the musical luddites are missing the point: technology can be used for good or for evil, and in the right hands it's an incredible thing. And you can use it for more than just making the odd bleep: you can create new types of music, design your own promotional materials, and even make your own video.

In this book, you'll discover the different ways in which technology can benefit you. We'll look at sampling and sequencing, hard disk recording and computer music, but we'll also discover the technology that's available to guitarists and singers. It doesn't matter whether you're into hip-hop, house or extreme noise terror: in the following pages you'll find out how the latest kit can help you turn your ideas into reality.

But technology isn't just about making music: it can help you promote your music too. In the later chapters of the book we'll look at some of the ways you can turn technology to your advantage, from digital photography and desktop publishing to the technology that you can use to make your own videos or electronic press kits. We'll also discover the dark side of technology: why you can guarantee that things will break at the worst possible moment, the precautions you should take before playing live, and what you can do if your hardware hates you.

This book won't teach you how to build a sampler using bits of string and sealing wax, and it won't cover dull stuff such as programming computers. What it will show you is the sheer range of musical technology that's available – and what's likely to work for you.

CHAPTER 1: WE HAVE THE TECHNOLOGY

From guitar gods to bedroom techno overlords, modern musicians are using technology in all kinds of ways. You'll find that use of technology tends to fall into three categories (although there's some overlap between them): creating music, recording music and performing music.

CREATING MUSIC

When it comes to creating music, you're spoilt for choice. Technology can be an instrument in its own right: samplers can chop up other people's songs, loop them and turn the results into something new; computers can control drum machines, keyboards and other hardware; software enables you to edit song ideas, add additional instruments or generate brand-new sounds; and there's a huge range of hardware that does everything from beefing up guitar sounds to triggering samples.

Although dance music is the most obviously mechanised form of music, that doesn't mean other types of musicians can't benefit. Technology turns up in rap and rock records, R&B, heavy metal and Nu-metal, and it even turns up in the classical world: for example, **Madonna** producer **William Orbit's** *Pieces In A Modern Style* combined well-known classical scores with the latest digital technology.

RECORDING MUSIC

One of the most exciting forms of music technology is in the world of recording. It's now possible to create entire albums on a computer and burn the finished tunes onto compact disc: **Radiohead** created most of their recent music on **Apple** *PowerBooks*, while the **ProTools** system is used by rappers, rockers and romantic types alike. Bands are discovering that instead of shelling out hundreds of pounds on professional studio recording, they can get decent results with a computer or a digital multi-track, and even big-name artists are embracing hard disk editing and other forms of technical trickery.

PERFORMING MUSIC

'Real' musicians used to taunt technology fans: 'Ah, but can you do it live?' These days, the answer is an emphatic 'Yes'. Not only can you take technology on the road, but you can use it to do things that the luddites can only dream of. Guitarists can start and stop sequenced melodies with foot pedals, while virtual guitars can emulate almost anything; drummers can trigger samples from behind the kit without sacrificing the meaty thump of real drums; singers can stick their voices through all kinds of effects, and keyboard players no longer need eight pairs of arms to play all their keyboard parts. Using different sounds no longer requires a stage full of expensive – and fragile – gear, either: keyboards in particular can be switched from a **Rhodes** piano to a harpsichord and even a heavy metal guitar sound by pressing a few buttons.

TECHNO TECHNO TECHNO TECHNO

Technology is everywhere in music. To take just one example, fans of the ProTools studio system include rappers **Outkast**, Nu-metallers **POD**, gloomy goths **The Cure**, and everyone from R&B diva **Mary J. Blige** to pop muppet **Christina Aguilera**. Then there are the bands that use samplers, state-of-the-art guitar effects, MIDI triggers... the list is endless, but the following examples should give you a good idea of how powerful – and how flexible – music technology can be.

MOBY'S HOME WORK

Moby's album *Play* sampled old field recordings of blues artists, and teamed them up with his own dance beats. The album used a combination of the Cubase computer program and traditional studio equipment such as mixing desks, samplers and effects processors, but since then Moby has embraced computer technology almost exclusively.

As he told **Rolling Stone** magazine, 'Eventually, records will be made utilising just a laptop and a MIDI controller. The sound quality is already so good, and it's so much less expensive... The companies that make those big recording/studio mixing desks must be terrified. You can get a virtual desk for a few thousand dollars that does more than an $800,000 console.'

Play and its follow-up *18* were both recorded in **Moby's** home studio, which boasts a surprisingly modest collection of equipment: an **Apple Mac** running **Cubase** and **ProTools**; a couple of ADAT recorders; a standard mixing desk and a handful of samplers, sequencers and drum machines.

U2'S ENDLESS EFFECTS

For a rock guitarist, **U2's The Edge** uses an awful lot of technology. In addition to the usual collection of distortion pedals you'll find at most musicians' feet, the guitarist has employed a dizzying array of rack-mounted units including reverbs, delays and other effects processors;

virtual guitar systems such as **Roland's** VG-8; MIDI controllers; amp switchers; noise reduction systems; E-bows and pretty much anything you can imagine. Oh, and he plays keyboards too.

GORILLAZ GO APE

Sticking two fingers up at an increasingly image-obsessed music industry, **Blur's Damon Albarn** – and collaborators including **Tank Girl** creator **Jamie Hewlett** – developed a cartoon supergroup called **Gorillaz**. Each band member adopted pseudonyms, and were replaced in videos – and on stage – by cartoon characters. Thanks to some clever animated videos, a smart website and of course, some great music, Gorillaz' records sold by the truckload.

"I asked for Gorillaz not Gorillas, you idiot!"

COMING UP FROM THE STREETS

UK garage/rap sensation **The Streets**, AKA twentysomething brummie **Mike Skinner**, became the critics' darling with the release of his album *Original Pirate Material*. Recorded in his bedroom studio, the album employed a sampler and a collection of cheap and cheerful home recording equipment; to solve the difficult problem of getting a decent 'dead sound' for vocals, Skinner stuck a mattress in his wardrobe and recorded the vocals there.

RADIOHEAD'S TECHNO TOYS

If you listen to the electronica-influenced *Kid A* or *Amnesiac*, you won't be surprised to hear that **Radiohead** use a lot of technology in the recording studio. With a collection of **Power Macs** and **PowerBook** computers, the band uses **ProTools** for audio editing and recently switched from **Cubase** to **Logic Audio** for MIDI sequencing. **Logic** also plays a part in the recording process: the band's tour bus includes a Logic-equipped Mac that they use for multitrack recording whenever inspiration strikes. In an interview with **Rolling Stone**, **Radiohead** guitarist **Ed O'Brien** explains: 'It's our hottest studio toy at the moment. You can do hard disk digital recording on it. You can sample onto your computer, as opposed to having an external sampler. It makes it so easy to manipulate and create loops. It's basically an extraordinary box of toys.' The band's website (www.radiohead.com) is one of the most talked-about music sites on the Net, and they've even started using cheap technology in their videos: 'I Might Be Wrong' was shot and edited on a **PowerBook**.

PUBLIC ENEMY'S PUBLIC

The pioneering rappers **Public Enemy** have been at the forefront of digital technology, with firebrand frontman **Chuck D** one of the most vocal supporters of digital music and MP3 in particular. The band's 2002 album, *Revolverlution*, featured remixes by Net-savvy fans. The band made a capella versions of four songs available for download from their website (www.publicenemy.com), and encouraged fans to create their own remixes. More than 500 entries were received, and the best four mixes ended up on the album.

The above examples are all very different, but they have one key thing in common: musicians are making technology their own. From **The Edge's** world of guitars to **The Streets'** DIY recording and **Public Enemy's** remix-happy fanbase, technology is assisting musicians like never before. Over the next few chapters, we'll discover what sort of products are out there – and how they can help you turn your talent into tunes.

CHAPTER 2:
THE HARD BITS

There's a huge range of high-tech hardware to choose from, ranging from keyboards and drum machines to samplers and sequencers. Best of all, music hardware can talk to other music hardware or to computers, thanks to a technology called MIDI.

The most common bits of music hardware are keyboards, drum machines, samplers and sequencers. We'll take a quick look at what each type of hardware actually does, and then we'll discover why music and MIDI go so well together.

KEYBOARDS AND SYNTHS

The synthesiser (synth for short) revolutionised music. Instead of lugging grand pianos around, musicians could use synths: small, portable keyboards that could generate reasonable-sounding music. Over time they became cleverer, and became capable of generating ultra-realistic sounds – or completely weird sounds.

Without synths, the 1980s would have been much quieter and many genres of music – ambient, electronic, new wave and so on – wouldn't exist.

Today's synths/keyboards contain an incredible amount of processing power. For a few hundred quid you can get a keyboard with pressure-sensitive keys and a bank of sounds that recreates anything from a baby grand piano to a church organ or a choir. If the keyboard has a MIDI connection, you can also use it to control a sampler.

DRUM MACHINES

Unlike real drummers, drum machines don't get drunk, fall out with the guitarist, demand that one of their songs goes on the album, or start slow songs at insanely fast tempos. However, early drum machines were no substitute for the real thing: bands without drummers looked weird, and the drum sounds were obviously synthetic.

There's no such snobbery these days, and the technology has improved too. Modern drum machines use samples of real kits to generate amazingly lifelike drum sounds, and you can even add variation to the beat so that it has a more natural and less mechanical feel.

SAMPLERS

From rap to rock, sampling is everywhere. Samplers enable musicians to use 'samples' of sounds or records, looping them up and turning them into tunes, and the most famous sampler of all is the **Akai S1000** – which has appeared on records by **808 State**, **Nine Inch Nails**, **Moby**, **William Orbit** and pretty much any musician you can think of.

THE CUT THE CRAP! GUIDE TO: **MUSIC TECHNOLOGY**

These days a growing number of musicians use computer sampling software instead of dedicated samplers, but samplers such as the S1000 and its descendents are still a mainstay of many musicians' touring set-up.

SEQUENCERS

Sequencers such as **EMU's** *Proteus* series are dedicated bits of hardware that control MIDI instruments such as keyboards and drum machines. Songs are programmed into the sequencer (or loaded from disc), and the sequencer then tells the instruments what to play. As with samplers, computers have superseded sequencers in many home studios, but for touring musicians a sequencer is much less fragile, more powerful and more flexible than a computer running sampling software.

"Sorry, Ben, but this guy just rocks more than you..."

STUCK IN THE MIDI WITH YOU

MIDI is short for **Musical Instrument Digital Interface**, and it's a language that enables bits of musical equipment to talk to each other. It's exceptionally powerful: for example, you can connect a keyboard to a tone generator to get new sounds, or use a sequencer to control a keyboard and a drum machine.

MIDI-enabled hardware usually has three connections: **MIDI in**, **MIDI out**, and **MIDI thru**. As the name suggests, the **In** connection is for incoming data, for example from a sequencer or a computer; the **Out** connection is for outgoing data, for example if you're using a MIDI keyboard to control a sampler or tone generator. Finally the **Thru** connection sends an exact copy of the incoming MIDI data to another device. Data sent via the **Thru** connection isn't affected by anything you do on that particular device, so for example if you're playing a keyboard, anything you do won't be sent via the **Thru** port.

MIDI transmits 16 channels of data, each of which can specify a note, its volume, and dynamics such as attack and sustain. It's possible to connect up to 16 devices together, but that's not always a good idea: each channel represents an individual 'voice', and many bits of music hardware use several voices simultaneously. For example, drum machines need one voice for the kick drum, one for the snare, one for the hi-hat and so on – that's three MIDI voices for a pretty basic drum track.

THE CUT THE CRAP! GUIDE TO: **MUSIC TECHNOLOGY**

In addition to notes, MIDI can transmit system information. It can send a clock signal to ensure that all your devices keep to the same beat, and it can tell them when to start or stop a song.

The result of all this means that it's possible to control multiple devices – keyboards, tone generators, drum machines and so on – without growing ten extra pairs of arms.

GENERAL MIDI

General MIDI, or **GM**, is an update to the MIDI standard that's designed to ensure that MIDI music sounds roughly the same on different devices – so for example a song will sound the same on a keyboard as it would on a computer. To achieve this, GM hardware has a 'bank' of 128 standard sounds, which correspond to particular numbers – so a piano sound on one GM machine will be a piano sound on another GM machine. However, GM doesn't specify how hardware should render those sounds, so a piano sound on a computer will sound very different from one on an expensive MIDI keyboard.

MIDI IN ACTION

Example 1: Keyboards and sound modules

One common use of MIDI is in sound modules, MIDI-compatible bits of hardware that create specific sounds such as grand pianos, string sections and so on. It's one of the simplest ways to benefit from MIDI: when you play a note on your keyboard, it tells the sound module what note you played and how hard you hit the key. The sound module then turns that information into a sound. If you play a C and hit it hard, the sound module plays a loud C using your chosen sound; if you play a D quietly, the sound module plays a D quietly, and so on.

Example 2: Drum triggers

Even drummers can benefit from technology. You probably won't be able to persuade your drummer to swap his kit for an electronic one, but you can add MIDI triggers to an existing kit. These triggers work in a similar way to the keys on a MIDI keyboard: when your drummer smacks a trigger, it sends out MIDI data to say which trigger he hit and how hard he hit it. If the trigger is hooked up to a sound module or a sampler, then you'll get a sound.

Drum triggers are useful in a number of ways. You can add additional sounds to the drummer's repertoire, for example by adding more electronic sounds or some processed drum sounds; alternatively, you could use samples and have your drummer trigger the appropriate sample during a song.

Example 3: Everything connected to everything else

This is where things get really interesting. With the right software, a computer can control all kinds of devices. You could connect a sampler, a drum machine and a keyboard to your computer and control them all via MIDI, getting the best of both worlds: the ease of computer-based music and the sound quality of professional music gear. And computers can also combine recorded music – such as your own guitar and vocal tracks – with MIDI music, enabling you to create amazing music with a few clicks of a mouse.

Nigel suddenly realised he was having a mid-life crisis

ANALOGUE VS DIGITAL

One of the biggest controversies in the world of music is the analogue versus digital debate. Digital kit, claim the critics, sounds more clinical than analogue stuff – and they're right. The reason is that digital equipment is based on sampling, so instead of reproducing something exactly, digital equipment provides a reasonable facsimile of it. Modern digital equipment uses very high sampling rates so the average person wouldn't be able to tell the difference between an analogue and digital recording; however, for serious audiophiles there's still a dramatic difference.

The classic example of the analogue versus digital debate is CDs versus vinyl. Because of the way CDs work, they don't store as much information as vinyl records do – so while they're clearer-sounding, you often miss out on the 'warmth' you get with vinyl LPs. However, CDs don't suffer from pops, clicks or other annoying artefacts, and most of us now use CD for our music.

It's a similar story with music equipment. Analogue recording gear does sound less clinical than modern digital kit, but it also has its problems – in particular, tape hiss on cheaper models. Editing a song recorded on tape is much harder, too: with digital kit you can wave a mouse around to edit a song, but on analogue you need to cut the tape with razor blades and glue it back together if you want to combine several takes together. For sheer convenience you can't beat digital.

THE CUT THE CRAP! GUIDE TO: MUSIC TECHNOLOGY

The other key issues are portability and reliability. A synthesised **Fender Rhodes** piano doesn't sound quite as good as a real one, but the synth is likely to be more reliable and an awful lot easier to carry up a flight of stairs. When you then consider that that same synth can also emulate a church organ, a choir and a helicopter, the attraction of digital technology should be obvious – and that's before you start thinking about MIDI music or computer-based sequencing.

Another argument against digital technology is that it's more expensive than analogue technology. On the face of it, that seems true: a tape-based 4-track recorder is much cheaper than a digital 4-track. However, it's not a fair comparison: a digital 4-track offers significantly better sound quality, and often a number of editing features. And of course, digital gear gets more powerful every year, so a piece of hardware that costs £400 today

DIGITAL – PROS AND CONS

UPPERS

1. No loss of signal quality
2. Almost infinite levels of control and adjustment
3. No moving parts or valves to break down and replace
4. Extremely versatlie and compact
5. Integrates seemlessly with computers, sequencers and other hi-tech gear
6. Current technology can mimic almost any piece of analogue gear, from mics to guitar amps and valve compressors

DOWNERS

1. Possibly less 'warmth' to the sound, although this is very subjective, and modern digital gear has improved greatly
2. In the short term, can be more expensive

will be a fraction of that price within a year or two. It happened with CD players, DVD players and computers: early models cost a fortune and took up an entire building, while later models are cheap, reliable and portable.

There will always be purists who argue that a valve amplifier sounds better than a modern, solid state one; that a knackered old keyboard sounds better than a digital synth; that a tape-driven echo machine sounds better than a digital delay; that tape recordings are sonically superior to digital ones. And that's absolutely true, but in most cases the difference is very, very slight – and certainly not dramatic enough for the average listener to detect.

If you want the maximum flexibility with the minimum amount of headaches – and don't fancy giving yourself a hernia from lugging keyboard after keyboard into gigs – then digital gear is the way to go.

THE CUT THE CRAP! GUIDE TO: **MUSIC TECHNOLOGY**

CAN COMPUTERS COPE?

On the face of it, it looks like a computer is the best bit of hardware you can buy. In many cases that's true, because computers are incredibly flexible bits of kit – as we'll discover in later chapters. However, they're not always the best answer for every musician. In particular, computers' fragility is a problem: unlike rack-mounted samplers or sequencers, which tend to be built like tanks, computers break easily. They're also prone to crashing, a problem that generally doesn't affect dedicated hardware such as a sampler; and there's reliability to consider, too. When you're using a computer as a sampler and a sequencer, if it packs up you've lost two essential bits of equipment. As you'll discover in **Chapter 10**, if you're planning on relying on a computer you need to take a lot of potential problems into account.

If you're embarking on a gruelling world tour – and you've got plenty of money – then you're probably better off with dedicated hardware. If you're on a tight budget, go for a computer instead. With the right software it can do most of the things that stand-alone hardware can do – for a fraction of the price.

CHAPTER 3: GUITAR GEEKS

You don't need to be a keyboard whiz or a computer geek to benefit from digital technology. As legions of guitar players have discovered, even cheap kit can take spanking your plank to a whole new level.

You can simulate the sound of amplifiers that only **U2** can afford, or transform the sound of your instrument beyond all recognition. You can do this in four ways: with a MultiFX box, with a rack mount, or by using either an E-bow or a MIDI guitar. But first – preamps.

PREAMPS

Preamps – short for **preamplifiers** – are the simplest form of guitar technology, and you'll find them in many modern acoustic guitars. A preamplifier is just a little amplifier, and when it's built into an acoustic it enables you to tweak the sound before it goes to your amp (or more usually, to the PA system). Typical preamps give you control over the bass, middle and treble together with overall volume, which helps reduce on-stage feedback; more advanced models have more complicated EQ features that enable you to get a realistic acoustic sound at insane volumes.

MULTIFX

Multiple effects, or MultiFX for short, are floor-mounted units that replace traditional 'stomp boxes' – guitar pedals such as distortions, choruses and so on. For less than £100 it's possible to plug your guitar into something that emulates the sound of several different pedals, but if you spend a little more money you could end up with something rather special. Mid-range MultiFX units not only include stacks of different effects, but they also enable you to edit each type of effect to create new sounds. You'll also find advanced technology such as amp simulators, which can turn even the cheapest amp into something that sounds like a **Marshall** stack, a **Mesa Boogie** amp, or a knackered cassette recorder.

There are four things to look out for when you're considering which MultiFX unit to buy. The first – and this is the most important if you're planning to play live – is the build quality. All MultiFX units are not created equal, and a cheap and nasty plastic job will fall to bits much more quickly than a metal one. If your chosen MultiFX unit has a wah pedal and you intend to use it, then don't even consider a plastic one – they're not really up to the job of sustained wah-wah abuse.

The second thing to consider is the amount of control you have over effect settings. Does the MultiFX limit you to its own preset sounds, or can you create your own? Think about the way the system stores presets, too: it should be easy to save and recall any sounds you've saved. You don't want to interrupt a gig because you've no idea where your heavy metal sound is.

THE CUT THE CRAP! GUIDE TO: MUSIC TECHNOLOGY

Thirdly, you need to look at 'chaining'. Most MultiFX units enable you to create chains of effects, and there's usually a limit to how long a chain can be. Some units let you combine three different effects, others let you combine seven, but that's not the only issue: depending on the manufacturer, your MultiFX unit will only let you put certain types of effects together in a chain. So for example if you use a flanger in your chain, you won't be able to use a chorus as well; if you use a digital delay, you might not be able to use a reverb too.

The final thing to check is timing. Is there a noticeable delay when you switch between two different sounds? If there is, then the MultiFX unit will cause lots of headaches if you use it in a recording studio, or if you tend to switch between several different sounds in a single song. Generally speaking, the cheaper the unit, the more noticeable the delay will be. It's very important to test your potential purchase in the shop to see if you can live with the switching delay; if you can't, don't buy it.

TOP 6 GUITAR EFFECTS

1. Distortion
Everyone from Metallica to the Cardigans uses fuzz when they want to rock out!
2. Wah-wah
The funkiest effect know to man – check out 'Theme from Shaft' or Jimi Hendrix's 'Voodoo Chile'
3. Delay
U2's The Edge has built his trademark playing style around this atmospheric effect
4. Flange
Beloved of manky old goths everywhere
5. Reverb
Makes your guitar sound like you're playing in a cathedral – enough said!
6. Compression
Simply, it makes loud things quieter and quiet things louder

Another timing issue that you might want to consider is the timing of any digital delay settings. Can you adjust the delay speed quickly, for example if you're playing live and your drummer has started the song at too fast a tempo? Can you fine-tune the delay speed, or are you limited to a few hard-wired settings? Again, find out before you part with any of your hard-earned cash.

Rack mounts are MultiFX units on steroids. A typical rack mount comes in two parts: the effects processor itself, which sits on your amp or in a studio rack, and a floor controller that contains the pedals you use to control the sounds. Not all rack mounts contain multiple effects, though: some are dedicated to a single type of effect such as reverb, and provide every conceivable version of that effect. The up-side? You get complete control over every aspect of your sound – but rack mounts take up much more room than their smaller MultiFX equivalents, and cost a lot more. However, if sound quality is the most important feature for you, then you'll notice a big difference between the sound of a rack effect and that of a MultiFX box.

THE CUT THE CRAP! GUIDE TO: **MUSIC TECHNOLOGY**

E-BOW

Even if you haven't already used an E-bow, you've probably heard one. As you might be able to guess from the name, **REM's Peter Buck** uses an E-bow on the song 'E-bow The Letter', while **U2's The Edge** goes E-bow crazy on live versions of songs such as 'With Or Without You'. And you can't blame them: in the right hands, an E-bow is a fantastic gadget.

"I said e-bow, not pillow, you ee-jit!"

E-bow is short for **Electronic Bow**, and that's essentially what it is – although it uses electronics rather than horse hair to create a sound. The unit works by generating a magnetic field between the E-bow and your guitar's pickups, which vibrates the string at high speed. The result sounds as if you're playing the string with a bow rather than with a plectrum, and with a bit of practice you can make your guitar sound as if it's a cello.

In addition to traditional sounds, E-bows can also generate harmonics. Simply select the second setting on the E-bow's switch, and when you use it on your guitar you'll get a similar sound to the feedback you hear when your amplifier's far too loud.

An E-bow isn't cheap – expect to pay around £90 – but if you like the sustained guitar tones of REM or U2, then it's well worth having. It's a lot of fun, too.

MIDI GUITARS

Systems such as **Roland's VG** series take the idea of MultiFX one step further: instead of adding effects to the sound of your guitar, they can make it sound like a different instrument altogether. They do this by adding an extra pickup to your guitar – you can buy a new guitar with the pickup already fitted, or simply add one to your existing guitar – and connecting it to a fiendishly clever box of electronics.

THE CUT THE CRAP! GUIDE TO: **MUSIC TECHNOLOGY**

The key technology here is MIDI, which we've covered in previous chapters. Unlike normal pickups, MIDI guitar pickups turn what you play into MIDI data. This data is then processed by the main effects unit, and the result is anything you want. You can make your guitar sound like a string section or a keyboard, or you can get it to make strange and spooky noises.

The benefits of a MIDI guitar system are obvious: you can get the same kind of effects as a MIDI keyboard, without sacrificing the pose value of a typical electric guitar. However, there are downsides too: prices are steep (three or four times that of a decent MultiFX unit) and because the system doesn't work without its dedicated pickup, if you break a string onstage then you can't just swap guitars and pick up from where you left off.

Then again, it's still a damn sight better than those hideous guitar-shaped keyboards that infested the 1980s.

CHAPTER 4: COMPUTER MUSIC

The earliest personal computers were little more than glorified calculators, but today's machines are fantastic tools for musicians. With computers, you can explore the world of digital recording, emulate ancient instruments, or muck about with samplers and sequencers.

There are two main types of computer you can choose from: PCs running **Microsoft Windows**, or **Apple Macintosh** (Mac) computers. Both have their fans, but generally speaking a PC is a better all-round computer – however, if you're planning to use your computer for music and nothing else, then a Mac is a better bet, not least because Macs tend to be more reliable and easier to use than PCs. Ultimately the choice comes down to the software you want to use: **ProTools** is better on a Mac than on a PC, but programs such as **Sonic Foundry's** *Acid Pro* are PC only.

SAFE SPECS

Whatever type of machine you go for, you need to pay attention to four things: the processor; the hard disk; the memory; and the connections. Here's what you need to look out for.

PROCESSOR

This is the engine of a computer, and its speed is measured in Megahertz (MHz) or Gigahertz (GHz). A typical bottom-of-the-range PC runs at around 2GHz, or 2,000MHz; Macs start at just under the 1Ghz mark. However, Mac processors and PC processors are completely different beasts; as a rule of thumb, a 1 GHz Mac runs at roughly the same speed as a 2GHz PC. Go for the fastest you can afford.

MEMORY

Memory, or RAM (Random Access Memory) is measured in Megabytes (MB). 128MB of RAM is fine for word processing and accessing the Internet, but it's not enough for music: with less than 256MB of RAM, you'll encounter problems – especially if you're making multitrack music. Memory is relatively cheap, so get 512Mb of RAM if your budget stretches that far.

HARD DISK

The hard disk is where you store your files, and big is better: a CD-quality WAV file takes up around 10.5MB of space per minute of music, so a single three minute pop song will be 31.5Mb. And that's a finished song: if you're working with multitrack music, you'll have a separate WAV file for each instrument, so if you're using twelve-track recording that means 12 x 31.5MB, or 378MB of disk space. Remember that's per song, so if you're got a 12-

song album then you'll need 4,536MB (4.5GB) of disk space for your album. You'll also need space for software, system files and all the other stuff that computers need, so it makes sense to get the biggest (and fastest) hard disk you can afford.

CONNECTIONS

There's no point in having a fantastic computer if you can't connect to anything. Many music peripherals connect to computers' **USB** (Universal Serial Bus) ports, while more recent hardware uses **FireWire**, a super-fast type of connection. If you've got an older PC you can add USB or FireWire by installing cheap expansion cards; if you're shopping for a new system, look for one that has at least two USB ports and one FireWire port.

SOUND CARDS

Although almost every recent computer has a basic sound card that handles music and game effects, if you're serious about music then you'll need a serious sound card too. There's a huge range to choose from, and you'll find sound cards fall into one of three categories: all-rounders, MIDI cards, and recording cards.

ALL-ROUNDERS

As the name suggests, all-rounders can handle everything
– although they don't offer the same sonic performance or
MIDI functions of more expensive cards. But they do have
one thing in their favour, and that's price. You can pick up
a decent all-rounder such as the Sound Blaster Live for
around £50, and while it's not really up to the job of
serious MIDI composing or multitrack recording, it's fine
for basic home studio stuff such as loop-based music
creation.

All-rounder cards can also handle MIDI sounds, but the
available sounds tend to be fairly basic and unimpressive.
For best results, you'll need additional MIDI hardware – or
a dedicated MIDI sound card.

MIDI CARDS

MIDI cards such as **Yamaha's SW1000XG** aren't cheap –
expect to pay around £300 – but they're exceptionally
powerful musicians' tools. In the case of the Yamaha card
the outputs are gold-plated and there's no standard
speaker connection; if you want to hear your music you'll
need to connect it to your hi-fi system. On the card you'll
find a digital output, left and right phono outputs and a
dedicated MIDI port (not a combined MIDI/Joystick port
such as the ones you'll find on cheaper cards). A MIDI
cable is supplied, and there's a ribbon connector to attach
any expansion boards you decide to buy such as Yamaha's
dedicated digital mixing card.

THE CUT THE CRAP! GUIDE TO: **MUSIC TECHNOLOGY**

MIDI cards such as the **Yamaha** include a MIDI tone generator, and in the case of the SW1000XG that means more than 1,200 realistic sounds including pounding drums and crystal clear-bass guitars. The combination of a tone generator and decent sequencing software (which we'll talk about later in this chapter) makes it possible to create astonishing music without any additional hardware.

RECORDING CARDS

Some sound cards are aimed at the pro market, and offer high-quality sound and a number of features for serious musicians. Generally these offer better sampling rates (24-bit/96KHz sampling is common in pro cards), better-quality connectors, and in some cases you'll also get a breakout box. This is a box that connects to the sound card and provides additional inputs and outputs such as digital and optical connections, phono plugs for instruments, and so on. If you're planning on buying **ProTools**, this kind of card is included in the (rather scary) price tag, and **ProTools** won't run without it.

CHOOSING A SOUND CARD

Sound cards are not created equal. Some cards won't run with certain software (for example, some PC cards don't get on with **Windows XP**); others are great for electronic music and flaky for recording; still others require ridiculously powerful hardware. If you're considering a new card, do your homework: check out Internet sites such as **Harmony Central** (www.harmony-central.com) and **InterMusic** (www.intermusic.com), and get your hands on magazines such as **Computer Music** or **Future Music** to find out what their reviewers – and their readers – think of your proposed purchase.

SOFTWARE

Most sound cards come with a selection of software that you can use to make music, but the supplied programs tend to be demo versions that aren't worth much. For serious music making you're going to need serious software; depending on the sort music that you want to create, you might want to consider one of the following types of programs.

EMULATORS

Programs such as **Propellerheads'** *Rebirth* are emulators, which means that they emulate specific hardware – in this case, the cornerstones of Acid music: the **Roland 808** and **303**. Rebirth recreates them perfectly, enabling you to create suitably squelchy noises and beats that you can save for use in another program.

You'll also find emulation in pro-audio software such as **Cubase VST**. Its 'virtual instruments' are software programs that plug in to Cubase, enabling you to add bass guitars or well-known synths to your music without shelling out for hardware or having to record live instruments.

LOOP-BASED PROGRAMS

One of the easiest ways to make music is to build it from loops: choose some beats and basslines, move them around and voila! Instant tune! There are plenty of loop-based programs to choose from, but one of the best is **Sonic Foundry's** *Acid Pro*. In addition to loops, it can handle MIDI and multitrack music, and includes effects that you can use to change the sound of individual tracks. It's not cheap – it'll set you back more than £200 – but it's a great program.

PROFESSIONAL MUSIC PROGRAMS

When it comes to music, **ProTools** is the daddy. It's widely used in recording studios, is available for PCs and Macs, and enables you to record multi-track music, add effects and edit individual tracks. However, it's also incredibly expensive – and it's not the only program out there.

When it comes to professional music-making software, you're spoiled for choice. **Cubase VST** is a firm favourite on the PC and enables you to combine MIDI and live instruments, virtual instruments and effects; on the Mac, **Logic Audio** does something similar. **Cool Edit Pro** is a cheap and cheerful multitrack recording program, while **Sonic Foundry's** *Sound Forge* and **Steinberg's** *WaveLab* are designed for editing individual tracks and **GigaSampler** turns a PC into a sampler.

Before you shell out on serious software, head for the Internet: you can download 30-day trial versions of most music programs, and it's a good idea to make sure a program does what you want it to do (and that it suits your way of working) before you shell out any of your hard-earned cash.

TECH TRAPS

Making music with computers is a great thing, but it's possible to get things very wrong – especially if you get carried away. The following list details some of the issues you're likely to encounter.

Reverb is your friend

Every room has a slight echo to it, and if you're plugging instruments directly into a computer then you'll lose that 'natural reverb'. As a result, you'll have to use effects to add reverb to your recording, or it'll sound unnatural and lifeless.

Too many toys

Just because a program lets you put distortion, chorus, EQ, phasing, flanging, wah, modulation, echo, delay, pitch shifting and God knows what else on a track doesn't mean you should put these things on your track. Avoid the temptation to use every trick in the book on every recording: less is more.

Noise annoys

Recording is only part of the equation: if you've got cheap microphones, your recording will sound cheap; similarly, if you're connecting a mic directly to your sound card, it'll sound awful. For best results you'll need a decent (i.e. expensive) microphone and a pre-amp: connect the mic to the pre-amp, then the pre-amp to your sound card.

Live and loud

Home recording is best suited to 'quiet' music or electronic music: if you're trying to capture the thunder of a heavy metal band at full volume, it's not going to happen in your living room. For that, you'll need a studio.

"OK - here it is with flange, chorus, distortion, phaser and wah-wah all turned up to 11"

MONEY TALKS

Professional recording equipment is expensive, and so is professional computer recording equipment. It's possible to put together a system that's fine for making demos or CDs to sell at gigs for a few hundred quid, but if you want state-of-the-art sound quality you'll need to spend serious cash on professional sound cards, software and equipment: microphones, effects units and so on. You can do a lot with computers, but if you want to have the same computer kit you'll find in an expensive recording studio that means shelling out for a top-of-the-range Mac, ProTools, a proper mixing desk and a collection of effects. If that's what you need for the music you want to record, then you may be better off hiring a studio than trying to amass all the necessary equipment yourself.

CHAPTER 5: DIGITAL RECORDING

We've discovered how you can turn a humble PC into a home studio, but that's not the only way digital technology can help you with your music.

From simple portable recorders and multitracks to state-of-the-art studio systems, digital technology is everywhere.

I WANT MY MP3

Portable MP3 players are becoming popular, and 'jukebox' models can store thousands of MP3 music files – and many of them can record, too. Many jukebox recorders include line-in sockets that you can connect to a mixing desk, and you can record in CD quality WAV format for perfect reproduction. With several hours of recording time, jukebox recorders are a great way to preserve gigs or rehearsals for posterity.

MAGIC MULTITRACKS

The humble 4-track recorder has grown up, and digital versions are widely available. For less than £700 – and prices are falling fast – you can get a digital 4-track that dispenses with tape and uses an internal hard disk for recording, and many of them include editing features that you can use to chop up tracks, get rid of mistakes and generally tweak your recordings. For slightly more cash, you can get 8-track or even 16-track versions, and many digital multitracks include a CD writer that enables you to make your own CDs.

If you're considering a digital multitrack, pay close attention to the storage technology it uses: cheaper models rely on Zip discs, which can be pricey and don't give you a massive amount of storage space. Multitracks that use computer-style hard disks are more expensive, but they're much more flexible.

If you need something more ambitious than a portable multitrack, you'll find that technology has taken over the recording studio too. Tape-based systems are still available, but more and more studios are using digital recorders: ADAT machines, or hard disk recorders (stand-alone bits of recording equipment, not to be confused with normal computers). ADAT systems record digitally onto video tape, and while they're not as convenient as hard disk recorders they're much cheaper – and you don't need to worry about storage capacity, because you can buy more tapes.

Most ADAT and hard disk recorders can be chained together, so for example you can hook up two 8-track machines to a mixing desk and benefit from 16-track recording. However, such technology only makes sense in a 'proper' studio environment: unless you know your way around a recording studio and you've got a few thousand quid to spare, you'd be better off with a computer-based set-up. Even if you've got the expertise and the cash, digital might not be the answer: many professional recording engineers believe that digital is too clinical, and that tape-based systems deliver a 'warmer' sound.

THE CUT THE CRAP! GUIDE TO: MUSIC TECHNOLOGY

AUTOMATION

Technology is at its best when it makes your life easier, and a number of systems do just that. Tasks that used to take ages – or that required frantic button pressing – can be automated, and the benefits are available to anyone from the home computer user to the owner of a state-of-the-art studio.

The most impressive form of automation is called 'flying faders', and it's built into the kind of mixing desks that cost more than a car. It's impressive stuff: the engineer hits a button, plays the song, and moves faders and EQ controls around to get the right sounds in the right places. The desk records his or her movements, and can then play them back every time the song is replayed. It's quite spooky to watch, but for engineers it means they can do things that in the past would have required eight arms.

You can get similar benefits for considerably less cash if you use a computer-based music system. Music software can add fade-ins and fade-outs, and programs such as *Acid Pro* enable you to add 'envelopes' to individual tracks. Envelopes can be used to pan a track to the left and right, increase or decrease the volume, and in some cases to increase or decrease the level of an effect such as reverb, delay or distortion. It's not as easy as using a flying faders desk, but the results are similar.

Another way in which automation can benefit you is if your software can save presets. For example, you might have spent ages mucking about with EQs and effects to create a killer drum sound; many programs enable you to save those settings as presets. Once saved, you can call up the appropriate preset at any time – so if you're working on a new song, you can bring up the drum sound from another song with a couple of mouse clicks. You can also save presets in many effects, such as the ones in **Cubase VST**, with similar results: getting the perfect compression setting, the best distortion sound or the right level of reverb is just a matter of loading the appropriate preset into the program.

In addition to presets, computer-based systems enable you to save as many different versions of a song as you like. You can create different mixes or edits and save each one separately, which is handy if you're trying different ideas and don't want to lose your original mix.

Finally, programs such as **WaveLab** can carry out 'batch processing'. This means you can do the same thing to several files at once, such as applying the same effects to several different tracks. To do this it's just a matter of setting up the effects you want, choosing the sound files you want to apply the effects to, and hitting the OK button. The computer then goes through each file, applies the effects, and saves the results. To do the same thing manually would take hours; with a computer, you can do it in a matter of minutes.

BOOTLEGGING

Bootlegging – sticking two or more completely different songs together and putting the resulting MP3 on the Internet – received stacks of publicity recently, when an illegal bootleg based around a **Gary Numan** sample was remade – legally – by the **Sugababes** and the original bootlegger. Artists ranging from **Pink** to **Christina Aguilera**, **The Strokes** and **Missy Elliot** have all been mixed up by Internet bootleggers, and the record industry tends to turn a blind eye to such illegal antics. One bootlegger, Glaswegian artist **McSleaz**y (www.mcsleazy.co.uk), is apparently in negotiations with record companies to produce all kinds of mixes legally, while **Kylie Minogue** paid tribute to bootleggers at the 2002 Brit Awards by combining her own 'Can't Get You Out Of My Head' with **New Order's** 'Blue Monday'.

"Let's try a cross between Mozart and Napalm Death!"

Creating a bootleg is easy: all you need is Internet access, some editing software and a bit of talent. The first step is to log on to a file-sharing network such as **KaZaA** (www.kazaa.com) and look for a capella tracks, versions of songs without any music. If you're looking for a vocal then your best bet is dance or R&B music, as a capella versions of popular tracks are often made available to club DJs (and inevitably, uploaded to the Internet).

Once you've got your vocal, the next step is to find a suitable soundtrack. Recent examples include **Eminem** teamed up with **Britney Spears**, **Christina Aguilera** vs. **The Strokes**, and so on. Rock music is particularly good for a soundtrack, as most rock songs have a section where the song plays before the vocal kicks in – think **AC/DC's** 'Back In Black' or any recent rock record. Using your editing software it's easy to isolate the appropriate section of music, cut it up and turn it into a loop; you can then repeat the loop and stick the vocal on top. In a fairly short space of time you've got a teen-pop artist fronting a heavy metal band, or a rapper with Ukrainian folk music in the background. Once you've tweaked the track to your heart's content you can then export it as an MP3 music file and stick it on the Internet.

Bootlegging is a lot of fun, but as a trend it's already over: the music and style press have already pronounced that bootlegging is 'dead'. However, hundreds of Internet musicians disagree, and the bootleg scene is still thriving – as you'll see if you check out **Boom Selection** (www.boomselection.net).

THE CUT THE CRAP! GUIDE TO: MUSIC TECHNOLOGY

To date, the record industry doesn't seem particularly bothered by the bootlegging phenomenon; that's probably because bootlegs generate valuable word-of-mouth publicity for the artists. However, it's worth bearing in mind that bootlegging involves copyright infringement, which is a criminal offence: if you attempt to profit from other people's work, for example by charging people to download bootlegs, don't be surprised if industry lawyers come knocking on your door.

CHAPTER 6:
TOP TWEAKS

So far we've looked at the ways in which technology can help you create and record your music, but you can also use it to change your music altogether.

With the right kit you can turn a tuneless oaf into a professional singer, fix a dodgy performance or even create a whole new song from a couple of bars.

HARD DISK EDITING

For many musicians, hard disk editing is a godsend – and some artists wouldn't have a career without it. Hard disk editing is a spin-off from hard disk recording, and it's based on a simple idea: if a piece of music is stored as a computer file, then you can use a computer to muck about with it.

Editing is often used to fix performances, from simple tweaks (adding a fade at the end, getting rid of unwanted clicks and so on) to serious surgery. Purists may scream in horror, but it's the surgery that's the most interesting bit.

Let's say for example that you've recorded a song and the singer's performance was a bit erratic. The verses are okay, but the last chorus was a bit ropey. Rather than redo it, you can edit it. Nip along to the first chorus, copy it, nip along to the last chorus and paste. Easy!

That's a simple example, but you can do much more with hard disk editing. You can increase the volume, pitch or tempo of a track (or an entire song); cut bits out and rearrange the order of verses, choruses and so on, or you can do a bit of 'comping'. That's when you look at a bunch of takes – vocals are the most common things to be comped, but you can do it with anything – and find the best bits. So you'll use take 1 for the first line, take 23 for the second, take 9 for the third, and so on. Assembling the bits you want and sticking them together means you've created a composite take, or a comp. Dishonest? Maybe: after all, the singer did do all the lines in the song – he just didn't do them all in the same take.

If you can record it, you can edit it. Kick drum a little out of time? A few mouse clicks, and it's fixed. Guitar sound a bit too weedy? Copy the track, add a different EQ to the copy, and you've now got two guitars instead of one. And so on. The possibilities are endless – although it's equally possible for you to spend 16 hours comping a vocal when it might have been easier to kick the singer and order him to redo the vocal properly.

Hard disk editing isn't just limited to individual tracks or songs, though. With a bit of cutting and pasting and perhaps a bit of crossfading, you can stick several songs together – or build an entirely new song from various ideas you recorded earlier.

AUTOTUNE

If it weren't for AutoTune, many of today's B-list celebrities wouldn't have careers. AutoTune is a computer program that plugs into the **ProTools** system and fixes dodgy vocals. If the singer's a bit flat, AutoTune raises the pitch until the vocal is in tune again. If it's too sharp, AutoTune intervenes again to save everyone's ears.

It's incredibly clever and really does work – although it's sobering to think that the combination of AutoTune and hard disk editing means that many chart hits are performed by people who've never actually sang their own songs properly. We won't tell you who those artists are, but here's a clue: the same artists who use AutoTune tend to promote their songs by appearing half-naked in men's magazines.

RESTORATION

One of the most exciting things about digital technology is the way it can restore old recordings to their original glory – either to re-release them, or to sample them for use in another recording. Using a box of tricks that includes EQs, band pass filters and specially written software, it's possible to remove noise and other problems from old recordings, 'cleaning up' the sound so that it sounds fresh and new.

The same technology is even appearing in consumer software. Many CD burning programs enable you to copy old vinyl records or tapes to CD, and include technology that improves the sound quality. Declickers get rid of vinyl scratches, rumble filters get rid of the hum from some turntables, and band pass filters can get rid of the hiss that affects recordings on cassette tape. Although these programs are designed for CD burning, you can use the same features to create a WAV file that you can then import into your music software. Alternatively, you can invest in professional sound editing software such as **Sound Forge**, which goes a step further and enables you to carry out all kinds of sonic surgery. The program also supports plugins – little software programs that 'plug in' to your program and add new features – for fixing dodgy recordings.

CHANGING THE STYLE

If you're making multitrack music, it's easy to do a song in a different style or at a different tempo. For example, you might have created a rock song, but if you've mixed it on your computer you can then remove instruments and add new ones. The live drums could be replaced by programmed ones; bass guitars by acid-style bleeps and squelches; the lead guitar by a keyboard line. Changing the tempo is a matter of a few mouse clicks and voilà! Your hard rock epic is reborn as a banging dance anthem!

MASTERING

Mastering is the process of turning all your finished tracks into something that's ready to go to the pressing plant. That involves four things: topping and tailing, sorting out the volume, adding EQ or compression, and creating the final master. Needless to say, you can do it with computers: programs such as **Sound Forge**, **WaveLab** or **Steinberg Mastering Unit** can do all the work for you.

Topping and tailing means fixing the beginning and the end of each track. That could mean adding a long fade at the end of the song, or getting rid of the drummer's shouted 'wuntoofreefar!' at the beginning of it. You should also look for 'spikes' – unwanted clicks and pops that occasionally crop up on recordings – and get shot of them.

If you've got more than one song, you need to have sensible volumes for each track. Mastering engineers will increase the volume of tracks that are too quiet, and reduce the volume of those that are too loud. It's not just an aesthetic thing (although that's important too) – unlike tape, digital music (such as CDs) can't be driven too loud or you'll get what's known by engineers as 'clipping distortion', a nasty and abrasive clicking that makes your ears bleed and blows up speakers. There's some overlap between this and compression, because compressors are one way of preventing the volume from exceeding the maximum. If mastered correctly, the volume of your CD shouldn't change dramatically between songs.

Through a combination of EQ (equalisation), compression, stereo expanders, DeEssing and other effects, you can also make your song sound bigger, punchier and brighter. EQ is used to make the bass louder or the treble less harsh. Needless to say, mastering software doesn't just have a tone control – it can isolate and boost specific frequencies that are audible only to dogs, or remove the low-frequency rumble that makes the bass sound a bit too boomy. There shouldn't be too much variation in EQ between different songs – you should aim to keep a certain amount of stylistic consistency across an album, for example.

Compression boosts certain frequencies and limits others, or boosts the overall volume of a track. For example, heavy compression makes distorted guitars sound massive. It's also great on drums. It's very difficult to describe; it makes a song sound louder, and you'll hear it used on anything from Britney Spears to Limp Bizkit records. It can also be overused: if a song's over-compressed it makes you feel as if your ears are popping. Many records also use a thing called an 'exciter', which adds harmonics to the high frequencies of your song. It makes things sound brighter, but again it can be overused.

Other tricks include stereo expanders, which make the mix sound 'wider', more spacious and epic, DeEssers, which remove the nasty 'tsssssss' sounds (called 'sibilants') from vocals, and all kinds of reverbs and other effects. As with all mastering tricks, the trick is to be subtle rather than to turn everything up to eleven. In the case of sibilants on your vocal or low-frequency rumble on the bass guitar, you really need to sort that out in the mix rather than rely on the mastering program to fix it at a later stage – any effects applied during mastering apply to the entire song, so it's much better to sort these problems out during the recording/mixing stage.

If you're considering investing in mastering software, it's important to be aware of your own limitations. It's perfectly possible to load up your computer with compressors, DeEssers, limiters and God knows what else, but if your ears aren't up to the job then you're better off leaving it to the pros. The most important thing about a mastering studio isn't the software, or the number of compressors, or the price tag on the newly purchased mixing desk; it's the ears of the engineer.

CHAPTER 7: THE CAMERA NEVER LIES

These days, an artist's image is almost as important as the music – and in pop music, it's probably more important. When was the last time a pig-faced horse frightener got to number one in the charts?

Image isn't just about how you look – it's about how you present your music to the world. With a digital camera and a bit of computer equipment, you can make your own promotional materials such as posters or flyers, or you can create the artwork for your records. You can also manipulate photographs, for example to make them look better or to create complete fabrications.

IMAGE EDITING

In the world of image editing, **Photoshop** is king. This computer program is responsible for most of the images you see: magazine covers, CD packaging, even cornflake boxes. With **Photoshop** (or a cheaper equivalent such as **Paint Shop Pro**) you can take a photograph and adjust the colour, fix problems such as red-eye (the slightly alarming effect you get when you take pictures using a camera flash, and everybody in the shot ends up with spooky red eyes), or tell complete lies. For example, magazine covers are regularly edited in **Photoshop** to remove spots, or to stretch the image to make someone look thinner. It's also possible to combine two completely different images, for example by pasting people from one image into another one. With a bit of mucking about, your band could be headlining JFK stadium when in reality you're playing in the back room of the Dog and Duck.

DESKTOP PUBLISHING

Not so long ago, if you wanted to create printed materials – posters, flyers, and so on – then you had to pay a designer stacks of money and then pay a printing firm even more money. These days, all you need is a computer, a printer and some desktop publishing software.

The software you need ranges from the dirt-cheap (**Serif's** *PagePlus*, from www.serifsoftware.com) to the insanely expensive (**Quark Xpress**, from www.quark.com). But no matter how modest your budget, desktop publishing enables you to combine text and images to create your own artwork, which you can then print yourself on a home printer. You can use the same software to create artwork for professional printing companies, for example when you want to design your own artwork for CDs.

It's tempting to run off your own posters and flyers at home, but it might cost more than you think. If your printer uses ink, it'll cost you several pence per page – and in most cases, using a printing firm will work out cheaper.

If you're creating artwork for someone else to use, speak to your chosen company before you start designing. Most printing firms will have guidelines they can send you, and which tell you exactly what they need from you. It's very important that you submit your artwork in a format that the printing firm can read – most firms will charge you extra if they have to muck about with your designs – and make sure they send you a 'proof' before they start printing your work.

"The cover's great, but could you make me look a bit more like Madonna?"

A proof is a copy of your finished artwork that shows exactly what the end result will be, and you might be surprised by it: what looks good on a computer screen doesn't always look good on paper, and images that looked all right in your desktop publishing software might appear 'blocky' if they were low-quality pictures. Never, ever get anything printed without first seeing a proof: it's too late to make any changes once the printing firm has run off 1,000 copies.

PUBLIC IMAGE

If you'd rather not inflict your features on the general public – because you're shy, or because one of your band members fell out of the ugly tree, hit every branch on the way down and landed in the ugly swamp – the digital imaging can be used to create your entire image. Bands such as techno boffins **Underworld** make extensive use of computer graphics in their promotional materials, including photographs, to disguise the fact that they aren't the prettiest artists in the world. Other artists go one step further: as we discovered in chapter one, **Damon Albarn** and friends invented a fictional band called **Gorillaz**, with computer-animated cartoon characters in place of 'real' musicians. You could do the same with a copy of an animation program such as **Flash**, which is now easy enough for non-artists to use.

THE CUT THE CRAP! GUIDE TO: MUSIC TECHNOLOGY

NET BENEFITS

If you supplement your graphics software with some basic Web design software, you can use the Internet to promote yourself too. These days most bands are online, and there's no reason why you shouldn't also get on the Net – but if you do, try to avoid the bland brochure-style sites that so many musicians seem hell-bent on publishing.

A decent site will make people interested in what you're up to, and once they're interested you've got a good chance of persuading them to download your MP3 files or order (and pay for) your CD. Printing in-jokes, rants about gig promoters, your opinions on Marxism or a bland list of every gig you've ever played is likely to bore your site visitors to tears.

The Internet is an amazing thing for musicians, but it's a big subject that deserves a book in its own right. For an in-depth look at the power of the Net and how you can harness it for your own world domination plan, check out this book's companion title: **The Cut The Crap Guide To Music On The Internet**.

CHAPTER 8: MAKING MOVIES

Technology has revolutionised the world of music, and it's poised to do the same with video. Hardware and software companies believe that home video editing is the next big thing in the world of computers.

Soon it will be possible to edit your own movies on even the humblest home computer. For musicians, that means not only can you make your own music, but you can take care of the visuals too.

WHAT YOU NEED

To make your own videos you need a suitable computer and a video camera. For best results the computer and camera should have a **FireWire** (also called **iLink**) connection, which is designed to transfer video digitally; however, you can also use an older computer and an analogue camcorder by investing in a video capture card. This adds video connectors to your computer and enables you to take footage from a camera, muck around with it on your computer and then transfer it back to video tape.

If you've got a reasonably recent computer, all the software you need is already installed: on Macs, you get the wonderful **iMovie**, which makes it simple to edit video footage and add a soundtrack; on PCs, you get the rather less wonderful – but still useful – **Windows Movie Maker**. PC users who want something a bit more adventurous should check out programs such as **MGI's VideoWave**, which often comes bundled with video capture cards.

iMovie and **Windows Movie Maker** are fine for simple tasks such as basic video editing, but if you're looking for serious video editing software then a program such as **Final Cut Pro** (Mac) or **Adobe Premiere** (Windows or Mac) will set you back a few hundred pounds. You'll also need some serious hardware to run the software: it's designed for professionals rather than video beginners. If you're new to computer video, stick with **iMovie** or **Movie Maker**.

Once you've got your footage into the computer, you can do a number of things to it. You can edit the footage to match your music, and you can add text, special effects and fades, or change the colour – for example, by turning colour clips into black and white. Once you've saved the finished result, you can export it back to your camera via FireWire or your capture card; alternatively, you can keep it on the computer and make your own video CDs, DVDs or enhanced CDs. You can even stick your video on the Internet.

PUTTING IT OUT

Most computers come with a CD burner, a drive that you can use to make your own CDs and which comes with software that turns files into discs. You can use that software to create Video CDs, a technology that's similar to DVD movies but which uses standard blank CD-R discs. The quality isn't close to DVD but it's a cheap way to distribute video clips, and the discs will play on most DVD players and computers.

Enhanced CDs are slightly different. These are CDs that are formatted so that a normal CD player thinks they're music CDs, but they also hold video clips that computer users can access. Again, the software that came with your CD burner can usually create enhanced CDs, although you'll need to think carefully about the type of computer files you use – some types of video file won't play on every computer. If you're new to the world of computer video, we'd recommend giving Enhanced CDs a wide berth.

The third option is DVD. It's now possible to buy DVD burners, which work just like CD burners but which use recordable DVD discs. They're much more expensive than CD-R discs and the hardware comes with a hefty price tag, but if you want to make DVD movie discs that people can play in normal DVD players then they're very handy – especially if you've got a Mac. Apple's free iDVD software enables you to create menus and burn DVDs from your video footage – and you don't have to be a computer expert to use it.

VIDEO ON THE NET

Video CDs and DVDs are handy if you're planning to post your videos to people, but if you want the widest possible audience for your clips then it's a good idea to put them on the Internet. But it's important to think before you start putting video on the Net: the files are massive, so if your Web space provider limits the amount of data you transfer each month, it could cost you a fortune. To make a video file small enough to download in ten minutes, the picture will be tiny; unless you're catering for people with super-fast broadband connections, video is probably more trouble than it's worth.

If you've decided that Internet video is still for you, then you need to choose a suitable technology. There are two types of video on the Internet – streaming and download – and several different technologies that do both.

Creating clips for downloading is simple: choose the format you want to use, download the necessary software (called an encoder), and turn your video footage into the type of file you want. And that's it: stick it up on the Web, link to it from a Web page, and people can download the file to their computers. However, video clips can take forever to download, so if you want to provide instant gratification then streaming is the way to go.

Streaming is a fiendishly clever technology that chops a clip up into chunks; instead of downloading the whole thing, the user can watch the clip as it downloads. Quality is dependent on the type of connection the user has, though: watching video on a modem connection is a painful experience, and even broadband users have to content themselves with a tiny video window.

In practice it's a good idea to offer both types of video: a low-quality streaming version that people can use to preview the clip, and a full-quality version for download.

"A tragic case of waiting for video to download..."

To create these clips, you'll probably use one of the following technologies:

RealVideo
www.real.com

RealVideo has been around forever, and the necessary encoding software is free. You can use it to provide both streaming and downloadable video, and it's widely supported.

Windows Media
www.windowsmedia.com

Developed as a rival to **RealVideo**, **Windows Media** is Microsoft's attempt to provide decent multimedia software. Like **RealVideo** the encoding tools are free, and you can provide streaming and downloadable clips. However, at the time of writing Microsoft is viewed with some suspicion by many Net users so if you use **Windows Media** it's a good idea to use **RealVideo** as well.

QuickTime
www.apple.com/quicktime

Apple's **QuickTime** technology is the standard for video on Mac computers, and you can use it for streaming and downloads. It's great for users with super-fast broadband connections and the results are impressive, but unless you're catering for a Mac-only audience (which is unlikely: Macs account for just 5% of computer sales) it's probably not the best format for your clips as the streaming can be flaky for Windows users. Encoding software will cost you, too: although programs such as **iMovie** can export in **QuickTime** format, you don't get any real control over the output. For that, you'll have to shell out for more expensive video software.

DIVX

www.divx.com

DIVX uses similar technology to Apple's **QuickTime**, and is a familiar sight on file-sharing systems such as **KaZaA**. However, it's not widely used by non-geeks and there isn't a big choice of software for creating **DIVX** files, so it's unlikely to be the ideal format for your footage – at least, not for now.

Flash

www.macromedia.com

Flash was originally used for animation, and it's still the best animation package you can get. However, recent releases also support video, and while it's not as simple as encoding **RealVideo** or **Windows Media**, with **Flash** you've got widespread support (98% of Internet users have the **Flash** plugin) and the ability to create your entire website in the format. For animation it's the best format out there, but for the time being we'd recommend **RealVideo** or **Windows Media** if you want to add video to an existing site.

CHAPTER 9:
ONE STEP BEYOND

We've covered photography and video, but you can also use computer technology in other ways: to promote yourself to the press, to get your music to a wider audience, and to make music across continents.

ELECTRONIC PRESS KITS

Electronic Press Kits are designed for journalists, and usually combine live footage or an artist's music with additional information such as video interviews, biographical details or tour dates. In the past, EPKs were distributed on video tape, but these days it's possible to distribute them on the Internet or on CD discs. If you want your EPK to look professional, you'll need to use a multimedia authoring tool such as **Macromedia Director** (www.macromedia.com), the choice of professional multimedia designers.

GAMES

The market for computer games is huge, and canny record companies are beginning to realise that if they can get their artists on a game soundtrack, they could recruit a legion of new fans.

Most big-name games companies now deal directly with record companies, which is why you'll find artists such as **Nine Inch Nails' Trent Reznor** soundtracking action games, but some of them will consider music from unsigned acts – although the music needs to be appropriate for the game, so for action games the designer is likely to expect heavy metal or dance music.

RINGTONES

Mobile phone ringtones are worth millions, and unsigned artists can hook up with a company such as **Mobiletones** (www.mobiletones.com) to provide their music in ringtone format from their website. In the not too distant future, mobile phones will be able to do more than just play weedy versions of songs: they'll be able to play CD-quality music too.

"Next up - a bangin' tune for all you hardcore clubbers"

THE CUT THE CRAP! GUIDE TO: MUSIC TECHNOLOGY

E-SINGLES

An E-single is an electronic single, and you can release
E-singles without the hassle of traditional record pressing
and distribution. You can create E-singles in all kinds of
ways, but the simplest is to make an MP3 file (see below)
available from your website. Alternatively you can add
video or animation using a program such as Flash or
Director, and use your E-single to encourage people to buy
a real version in the shops. Irish band **The 4 of Us**
(www.the4ofus.com) have used this approach, and you'll
find a number of E-singles on their website.

MP3

MP3 has completely changed the world of music. MP3
files are songs that have been turned into computer files,
and they're small enough to be downloaded from the
Internet. The software you need to make them is free from
companies such as **MusicMatch** (www.musicmatch.com),
Real Networks (www.real.com) and **Microsoft**
(www.microsoft.com), and it's a doddle to use.

Putting MP3s up on your website is very important,
because it gives people an opportunity to hear your music
– and if they like it, you can probably persuade them to
buy your records. Be wary, though: if you put your entire
album on the Internet and people can download the whole
thing for nothing, then there's no reason for them to buy
the CD as well. Make one or two songs available for free,
and add a prominent link to your mail order page.

MP3 isn't the only technology for delivering music on the Internet (you can do similar things with **RealAudio, Windows Media** or a new contender, **Ogg Vorbis**) but it's by far the most widespread in terms of hardware and software support. More importantly, even non-computer users know about MP3 – something that can't be said for its competitors.

COLLABORATION

With technology, you can collaborate with musicians across the world. High-speed ISDN phone lines are frequently used to enable singers in the US to add their vocals to tracks being recorded in the UK, but even the most cash-strapped musicians can use technology to collaborate with far-flung colleagues. For example, you could record a drum track in MP3 and put it on your website, and a collaborator could import the drums into their music program, add a guitar part, and export the guitar as an MP3. Someone else could add vocals, bass, keyboards or rapping, and the resulting MP3 files can be assembled in a simple mixing program and made into a record. If you're having trouble finding like-minded souls in your local area, online collaboration means you can make records without having to travel around the world.

GENERATIVE MUSIC

Technology is normally used to assist musicians, but **Koan** (www.sseyo.com/koan) takes the musician out of the equation altogether. It's a 'generative music' program, which means that the software creates music from user-created rules or random events and data. The results are quite hypnotic, and legendary egghead **Brian Eno** – former **Roxy Music** star, father of ambient music and producer to **U2** and **David Bowie** – has even released whole albums of **Koan**-generated music. It isn't for everyone, but it's certainly fascinating stuff.

CHAPTER 10: WHEN TECHNOLOGY ATTACKS

In 2000, pop princess Britney Spears angrily denied claims that she didn't sing live – and looked like a right prat that night when, halfway through the show at Dallas's Smirnoff Music Centre, the vocal tape broke and rendered her silent.

Then there's **U2**, whose **Popmart** tour featured a giant lemon from which the band would descend to play an encore. Most of the time it worked perfectly, but in Oslo the lemon packed up and the band were trapped inside it.

The moral? Technology is like a dog. Most of the time it's your best friend, but from time to time it will leave something unpleasant on your carpet – and there's always a good chance that one day, it will turn around and bite you. Murphy's Law dictates that it'll happen when you really need everything to run smoothly: during an important gig, at a TV studio, or when you're up against an insanely tight deadline.

Technology can bite you in all kinds of ways, but these are the most common ones.

THINGS FALL APART

It doesn't take much to damage expensive musical hardware. Electronic equipment doesn't like it if it's too warm or too cold, and you can't throw kit around and expect it to work every time. Then there are connectors to consider: your keyboard might not have the right type of cables for a venue's PA system, or your mixer might use phono plugs when the PA system expects 3.5mm jack plugs. If you're taking your technology with you, it's a good idea to carry adaptors so that no matter what sort of system the venue uses, you can connect your kit to it.

Cables of all kinds are particularly prone to failure, especially if you're moving them around a lot. They can snap internally, or the cable ends might fall apart; power cords can fail, or their fuses might blow. Always carry spare cables, fuses, batteries and other important items so that if a 10p fuse blows, it doesn't blow the gig as well. If you're using a typical 9v power supply for a keyboard or guitar pedal, be careful with the cable: the bit that connects to the plug tends to be very flimsy and is easily damaged.

Be particularly careful around computers. Even the toughest PC or Mac is a fragile beast, and it doesn't take much to damage it beyond repair. Gigs are a particular hazard, because computers are designed to be used in clean, dry places – not sweaty hell-holes packed to the rafters with drunks. A spilt can of beer can permanently cook your computer – as can dodgy power supplies in some venues. It's a very good idea to invest in a surge protector, a special power adaptor that irons out 'spikes' in the power supply. Although most appliances don't mind such spikes, they spell instant death for computer equipment and other fragile electronics.

One thing that many musicians tend to forget about is theft. A laptop computer is particularly easy to steal, and such machines fetch good prices on the black market. If you can't be sure your laptop is safe, don't let it out of your sight.

MURPHY'S LAW

Murphy's Law states that if anything can go wrong, it will go wrong – so the more you rely on your technology, the bigger the problem if things don't work the way they're supposed to. If you use tapes, DATs or MiniDiscs to provide backing, bring spare copies – and be prepared to improvise like crazy if anything goes wrong with the backing track. Wherever possible, avoid using taped vocals on stage; audiences tend to accept backing tapes for keyboards and other instruments, but taped vocals are generally a no-no unless you're using samples and you aren't pretending to have a real live vocalist.

It's tempting to guarantee a perfect performance from your singer by playing a studio recording through the speakers, but you're tempting fate.

CRASH AND BURN

Computers crash. Sometimes it's annoying, for example when your machine locks up and you have to restart it; other times, it's catastrophic. If you've spent hours tweaking a track and you haven't saved it, a crash means you've lost all of your hard work; sometimes, a crashing computer can even destroy saved files if you were using them at the time of the crash. If those files represent six months of recording and mixing, you've got a problem.

With computers, it's a good idea to assume that it's just a matter of time before something goes seriously wrong. It's going to happen, so make sure you're prepared for it. Keep backup copies of everything, from individual loops to finished tracks, and keep them somewhere safe. Ideally they should be stored off-site, so that if your hardware explodes – or if someone breaks into your house and nicks it – you won't have lost all your work too.

Think about insurance, too. Put all your music gear and your computer hardware on your home insurance, and if you're taking gear out on the road then invest in decent flight cases and consider taking out additional insurance from a specialist insurer. A computer or sampler is much more fragile than a drum kit, and it doesn't take much to break it, so treat them carefully when you're gigging.

THE CUT THE CRAP! GUIDE TO: **MUSIC TECHNOLOGY**

INJURY TIME

One of the worst things about technology – in particular, computer technology – is RSI, or **Repetitive Strain Injury.** RSI isn't a single condition; rather, it's a catch-all term for a number of different injuries that are caused by making the same movements again and again. Tennis elbow is an RSI; so is housemaid's knee. With technology, the RSI to watch out for is carpal tunnel syndrome.

Carpal tunnel syndrome is usually a result of excessive keyboard and/or mouse use, and it's extremely unpleasant. You get it when the tendons in your wrist become worn, and untrained typists – people who use keyboards but haven't been trained in touch-typing – are particularly at risk from it.

A case of repetitive drone injury...

If you're the sort of person who plays very fast and who hits the keys particularly hard, then carpal tunnel syndrome is worth watching out for. In extreme cases, carpal tunnel syndrome can make it impossible for you to work – and even simple tasks such as lifting a kettle can be very painful.

The only way to prevent RSIs is to avoid the activities that cause them, which is hardly practical for computer musicians. However, there are some warning signs. If you tend to suffer from aches and pains after a protracted session at the computer, you should consider that as a fairly big hint and change your behaviour accordingly. That means taking regular breaks and keeping an eye on how long you're using your gear for; if you're the sort of person who regularly spends 10 hours in front of a screen, then it's not so much a question of 'Will you get RSI?' as 'WHEN will you get RSI?'

If you do find yourself suffering from RSI-style symptoms, don't make the mistake of popping a few painkillers and going back to work. Pain is your body's way of telling you there's a problem, and painkillers don't stop the damage. If anything, they can make the problem worse because you're continuing to work long after your body's screaming at you to stop.

For more information about preventing or coping with RSI, check out the **UK RSI Association** at www.rsi.org.uk.

CHAPTER 11: THE TEN COMMANDMENTS

Technology is a wonderful thing, but it has its downsides. It can be overpriced; it might stop working when you really need it to be reliable; it can refuse to talk to your existing hardware, and so on.

If you're thinking of investing in some high-tech gear, keep the Ten Commandments in mind and you should avoid the most common pitfalls.

1. THOU SHALT DO YOUR HOMEWORK

Whether you're looking for an effects rack or buying an entire system for hard disk recording, it pays to plan ahead. Read everything you can on the type of stuff you're planning to buy, and check out musicians' sites to find out what other people think of your planned purchases. With music software, you can usually get 30-day demo versions of even the biggest products; download them and try them out to make sure that they can do exactly what you want them to do. With keyboards, samplers or ProTools systems, make sure you get a hands-on demonstration before you part with any cash.

2. THOU SHALT STICK TO YOUR BUDGET

Whether you're in a music shop or checking out the sales pages on an Internet site, keep your wits about you: it's all too easy to spend a fortune on something you don't really need because of a pushy salesman or a particularly well-written bit of advertising copy. This is particularly true when buying computers: if you've decided on a particular specification, don't let yourself be persuaded by retailers to go for slightly more expensive models that come with goodies such as free software, bundled printers and so on. Nine times out of ten, you won't use the extra goodies and you'll have wasted your money.

3. THOU SHALT REMEMBER COMPATIBILITY

Some systems won't work with other ones. If you buy an Apple laptop, you can't take advantage of PC sound cards such as **Creative's** *Audigy* series; instead, you'll have to choose from a very limited range of products that hook up to your **USB** or **FireWire** ports. If you're running Windows, check the system requirements for software very carefully: some music programs will refuse to work with **Windows XP**, and it can be hard to get a refund. Compatibility is particularly important with older kit: some software programs won't work with older hardware, and it can be difficult to get spares or supplies for ancient recording hardware.

Think carefully about any equipment you've already got, and do some crystal-ball gazing so you've got an idea of the sorts of things you might want to buy in future. That way, when you buy new hardware or software you can be confident that it'll work with what you've got – and that it won't limit your choices when you buy gear in the future.

4. THOU SHALT NOT BE FOOLED BY FLASHING LIGHTS

When you pop into the local branch of **Dixon's**, you'll see stacks of hi-fi gear that looks incredibly high-tech but that seems amazingly cheap. Graphic equalisers are turned into dazzling on-screen displays, details are picked out in fluorescent blue, and so on.

"In the future all music will be beamed directly into our brains by lasers"

It's impressive stuff, but these systems are cheap for a reason: they're rubbish. LED lights don't make the slightest difference to the way a system sounds: that depends on the quality of the speakers and the quality of the components inside the system. You really do get what you pay for.

It's the same with music hardware. Don't be fooled by fancy displays, modern styling or anything else, because these things don't make the slightest difference to how your music sounds, how easy a bit of hardware is to use or whether a particular bit of kit is good value for money. It's like boy racers' cars: if you stick lots of spotlights, body kits and other bits and bobs onto a bog-standard Vauxhall Nova, it might look better – but it's still a crap car.

5. THOU SHALT NOT BUY VERSION 1.0

If you're considering buying a computer program and it's described as '1.0', run away. Software versions are described like this: 1.0, 1.1, 1.2 and so on. The first number is the version number, in this case version 1; the bit after the decimal point is the update number. So version 1.0 is the first ever release, version 1.1 is the first collection of bug fixes, and so on.

What that means in practice is that version 1.0 isn't close to being finished. There's a very good chance that it will stop working for no reason from time to time, and that it won't support the latest hardware. Wait for version 1.1 or later, or expect to spend a lot of time swearing.

6. THOU SHALT READ THE MANUALS

Male musicians are particularly bad for this. You've spent two thousand quid on a new keyboard that contains more computer power than a moon rocket, and the manufacturer has printed a 300-word book that tells you how it works. What do you do? If you're like most male musicians, you'll ignore the manual completely and start pressing buttons to see what happens.

There's nothing particularly wrong with the 'what does this button do?' method – unless you try it in a nuclear power station – but the manuals are there for a reason. If you ignore them, there's a very good chance that you'll be unaware of features that could inspire you to reach new heights, or that you'll end up spending 20 minutes trying to accomplish a task that should only take a few seconds.

7. THOU SHALT LOOK ON THE INTERNET

The Internet is an amazing resource for musicians. We've already mentioned looking for other people's opinions on your potential purchases, but the Internet's usefulness doesn't end when you've unwrapped your latest techno-toy. Software programs are updated regularly, and you can usually download these updates for free; there are sites that provide detailed information on everything from programming a keyboard to recording bands; you can download free samples and loops that you can use in your music, and for some programs such as Cubase VST you can get your hands on free or dirt-cheap effects and even virtual instruments.

Then there's the issue of technical support: if you've got popular hardware or software and you encounter a problem, someone somewhere has probably encountered the same problem already – and they may have found a way to fix it. You'll find such pearls of wisdom on manufacturers' message boards, on pro-audio forums and on the message boards attached to many music websites.

8. THOU SHALT NOT GET CARRIED AWAY

Technology is a tool, not an end in itself. What's really important is the music, so resist the temptation to use every technological trick you can think of in the first ten seconds of a song. Yes, it's possible to stick a wah, reverb, distortion, chorus, phaser, flanger, compressor, limiter, EQ, pitch shifter, octaver, harmoniser, ring modulator and God knows what else on a vocal track – but it'll sound rubbish. Be selective: you're supposed to be impressing people with your musical talent, not your encyclopaedic knowledge of special effects.

9. THOU SHALT NOT FORGET ABOUT COPYRIGHT

It's never been easier to nick other people's work and incorporate it into your own music, but unless you've got the creator's explicit permission then you're breaking the law. Uncleared samples – bits of other people's music you don't have permission to use – can be a nightmare for musicians, especially if you're releasing records. If you're not careful, you can end up owing a fortune in royalties to the people you've sampled – and in some cases, they could end up with all your money. When **The Verve** sampled the **Rolling Stones** for 'Bitter Sweet Symphony',**The Stones'** lawyers went ballistic; as a result, **The Verve** had to hand over every penny of their royalties. **The Beastie Boys** had to scrap plans to release 'Rock

Hard' because **AC/DC** wouldn't give them permission to use 'Back In Black', and **Public Enemy** scrapped 'Psycho Of Greed' because its **Beatles** sample would have cost millions.

When you're a musician, you're expecting people to pay you for the privilege of using your work – either by listening to it, or by putting it on records. In other words, you expect people to respect your copyrights, so you need to respect the copyrights of others. That means using legal copies of software, taking steps to get permission for any samples you use, and doing what you can to ensure that you're not ripping other people off. After all, why should someone pay for your music if you're not willing to pay for the use of others' music, or for the tools you use to make your tunes?

10. THOU SHALT CARRY SPARES

Things break, cables snap and batteries die – and Murphy's Law means that these things will happen at the worst possible time. If you're gigging, bring spares of everything: cables, batteries, connectors, anything that can possibly pack up, go missing or cause you problems. If you're using MiniDiscs or CD-Rs as backing tracks, bring duplicate copies; if you're running an entire set from a laptop computer, either bring a spare one or keep your fingers crossed that it won't pack up mid-set.

AFTERWORD: TECHNOLOGY ROCKS!

"From now on, whether or not the technology makes the traditional musician's craft redundant, the young creative type will become more aware that he is able to control more areas of the way his music is communicated to the masses. The manipulation of this control will become a very important creative form of expression in itself."
– The KLF, *The Manual: How to Have a Number One – The Easy Way*

Technology can be as big or as small as you want it to be. You can use it to record traditional instruments, or you can use it to elicit amazing new sounds from a simple guitar; you can conjure up an orchestra in your bedroom, or tweak the performance of a live drummer. Loop-based software means you can make music without first spending ten years learning to play an instrument, and sampling gives you the widest possible choice of the building blocks you use to make your music. And of course, entire genres of music – house, drum'n'bass, electronica – would be impossible without technology.

But the power of technology goes beyond making music. It enables you to control how your music is presented – from editing promotional pictures to making your own videos – and now, it can help you distribute your music too. Thanks to the Internet and MP3, you don't need a major record company behind you if you want people in Brazil to hear your tunes, and you don't need to spend thousands of quid on expensive record pressing if you want people to get their hands on your work. It's possible to write a song in the morning, record it in the afternoon and have people on the other side of the world listening to it by teatime.

Technology for technology's sake is very dull, and I doubt you'll ever persuade me to trade my **Telecaster** for a computer simulation of one. It's important to keep things in perspective: in the right hands the combination of keyboards, samplers, computers and effects can turn a great song into something truly exceptional, but the most high-tech option isn't always the best one.

For example, faced with a vocal sound he didn't like, **The Streets' Mike Skinner** went for the distinctly low-tech option of stuffing a mattress into a wardrobe to deaden the sound. What's important is finding technology that works for you, whether it's a fancy effects unit or a state-of-the-art computer system. But even more importantly, you need talent. If you've got that, then there's no limit to what you can achieve.

Gary Marshall

GLOSSARY: MUSIC TECHNOLOGY FROM A TO Z

The world of Music Technology can be a scary and confusing place – it's littered with acronyms, jargon, legalese and technical details. Most musicians find this incredibly difficult to deal with.

Fortunately for you, all the most important terms you're likely to come across are listed here, together with explanations that even a drummer could understand. If you find something in the main part of the book that you don't understand then check this section for clarification.

ADAT

Digital tapes used in recording studios. They look like video tapes, because that's exactly what they are – except instead of video, they're used to store music. It's magic!

ANALOGUE

Analogue equipment doesn't use silicon chips or other bits of high-tech hardware. Tape recorders are analogue; valve-powered microphones are analogue, and so on. Analogue kit is believed by many to deliver a better, 'warmer' sound than modern digital equipment, and bands often choose to record on analogue equipment in order to get the right, ahem, vibe.

See also: **Digital**

AUTOTUNE

Designed to work with the **ProTools** system, AutoTune is a fiendishly clever computer program that can take even the most tone-deaf bellowing and turn it into something that's nice to listen to. AutoTune is everywhere – especially on records by soap stars and other B-list celebrities.

BOOTLEG

Originally used to describe anything illegal from whisky to pirate CDs, bootlegging has developed a new meaning in the age of the Internet. An MP3 bootleg is a music file that's been made by sticking two completely different songs together, for example by combining an **Eminem** rap with the music of **The Strokes**. Most bootlegs are created without the copyright owners' permission, and while the music industry generally turns a blind eye to such tomfoolery, using other people's music is illegal and could land you in legal trouble.

THE CUT THE CRAP! GUIDE TO: **MUSIC TECHNOLOGY**

BOUNCE

With cheap four-track recorders you can 'bounce' existing tracks onto an empty one, for example by bouncing tracks 1, 2 and 3 onto track 4. You can then record over 1, 2 and 3 without losing the stuff you've already taped.

BROADBAND

Broadband is a catch-all term used to describe fast Internet connections. There are two main types of broadband: ADSL, and Cable. Both technologies offer speeds of around ten times faster than a standard modem connection, which means that an MP3 can be downloaded in a few seconds rather than a few minutes.

BYTES, KILOBYTES, MEGABYTES AND GIGABYTES

Computer storage is described in bytes (B), kilobytes (KB), megabytes (MB) and gigabytes (GB). One gigabyte equals 1,024 megabytes; one megabyte equals 1,024 kilobytes; 1 kilobyte is roughly equivalent to a page of A4 text.

CAMERA READY

When you're getting artwork done for your records, you'll often find that pressing plants expect your designs to be in camera ready format. This means that they want you to provide perfect copies of your artwork, which can then be scanned and used to produce the printing for your records. You can't create camera-ready artwork with a normal home printer; instead, you'll need to get a professional printing company to produce the artwork for you. Alternatively, provide your artwork as computer files on a CD-R.

See also: **Films**

CD-R, CD-RW

Recordable CDs designed for storing computer data but now widely used by bands and music pirates. CD-Rs are recordable only; CD-RW can be rewritten several times as if they were normal computer discs. For music, stick to CD-Rs.

COMPRESSION

Compression makes things sound louder by boosting the quiet bits and limiting the loud bits. You can get a compressor as a guitar pedal, but they're more commonly used by recording studios and radio stations to make music sound as loud as possible.

COPYRIGHT

Copyright law protects the people who create things; in music, that means you own the copyright on the recordings you've financed, and nobody is allowed to copy those recordings without your permission. With bands, the record company usually owns the copyright on the recordings, and a publishing company owns the copyright on the music.

CUBASE

Cubase is one of the most famous music programs, and it's used by artists such as **Radiohead**. Cubase can be used as a sequencer, for example to control keyboards and drum machines, or you can use its *Virtual Instruments* to recreate the sound of bass guitars and ancient synthesisers.

DAT

Digital Audio Tape is widely used in studios, because it provides CD-quality recording from the final mix (although it's in stereo rather than multi-track format, so you wouldn't use DAT for recording individual instruments). DAT tapes are regularly used as masters by pressing plants, but you won't find them in the high street: worried that people would use them to pirate CDs, the record industry effectively banned normal people from owning them in the 1980s.

DIGITAL

Digital equipment turns sound into computer data, which can then be tweaked in all kinds of ways. Digital equipment is generally smaller, cheaper and more reliable than analogue equipment, but purists reckon that it sounds clinical and lifeless compared to analogue gear. They may be right, but most of us still listen to music on digital CDs instead of analogue vinyl.

See also: **Analogue**

DRM

Short for **Digital Rights Management**, DRM is copy-protection technology that's designed to stop people stealing digital music files.

DVD

Video tape is dead, replaced by DVD – Digital Versatile Disc. Music DVDs offer pin-sharp picture quality and crystal clear sound, and quickly replaced music videos on the shelves of your local HMV.

See also: **DVD-A**

DVD-A

DVD-A discs – short for DVD Audio – offer ultra-high quality sound, often in surround sound. The record industry hopes that DVD-A will ultimately replace CD – although it has a competing format in the form of SA-CD.

See also: **SA-CD**

EBAY

Possibly the most addictive site on the Net, **EBay** (www.ebay.co.uk) enables you to auction your old stuff or buy other people's stuff. There's an amazing range of musical equipment on offer, including antique instruments, ancient recording gear and the latest digital kit. Like any auction, there are bargains to be found – but you have to be careful. People often suffer from auction fever, where they believe that auction sales are guaranteed bargains and end up paying more for a bit of old tat than they would for a brand new item in the high street. Fraud can be a problem, too, and of course you can't have a look at the items before you bid.

E-BOW

An E-bow is an electronic bow, a tiny – but pricey – gadget that uses magnetic fields to make a guitar string resonate as if you were playing it with a bow. You'll find E-bows all over records by **REM** and **U2**.

EQ

Short for Equalisation: cutting the bass, boosting the treble and so on.

FILMS

Printers make proof copies – final versions of artwork before they actually start printing – known as **Cromalin** films ('films' or 'chromes' for short). You'll need one film for each colour your artwork uses; most full-colour printing uses four colours – cyan, yellow, magenta and black. If your chosen pressing plant is also doing your artwork, make sure the cost of films is included in the price.

FLASH

More and more websites are designed in **Flash**, which you can use to create sites with animation, sound and even video. However, Flash works best on a broadband connection – and it's often used when HTML would be more appropriate. Before you decide to build a site in Flash instead of HTML, ask yourself whether the technology will actually make your site better. If it won't, don't use it.

FOUR-TRACK, 4-TRACK

Normal tape recorders are two-track: each side has a left channel and a right channel for stereo sound. Four-track recorders use both sides at once, which means you can record four instruments simultaneously. Newer machines don't use tapes at all: digital four-tracks use computer-style hard disks instead.

FX

Short for Effects. In the studio that means reverbs, delays, compressors and other studio marvels.

HARD DISK RECORDING

Recording that stores music on a computer-style hard disk rather than on tape. Hard disk recorders are available as stand-alone bits of music hardware, or you can turn a computer into a hard disk recorder using software such as **ProTools**.

KBPS

Short for kilobits per second – not kilobytes, as people often think – Kbps is used to describe the sampling rate of music files. To work out how much space a file will take up, you take the rate in kilobits and divide it by eight; this tells you how many kilobytes you'll need per second of music. So a three-minute song at 128Kbps takes up 2.8 megabytes (2,800 kilobytes); the same song at 192Kbps will need 4.3 megabytes. It's not very interesting, but it's worth knowing if you're short of Web space and need to cram a lot of songs into a small space.

MASTER

The Master – short for **Master Recording** – is the copy of your music that goes to the pressing plant and ends up on CDs, tape or vinyl. The process of creating the Master is known, cleverly, as Mastering.

MIDI

Musical Instrument Digital Interface, or MIDI for short, is a language that enables different bits of music hardware to communicate with each other. With MIDI, you can use a keyboard to trigger a sampler, or turn a guitar into something weird and scary.

General MIDI (GM) is an updated version of the MIDI standard, and it's designed to ensure that MIDI files sound roughly the same on different bits of hardware – so for example if one machine will play certain MIDI data as a drum pattern, then a different machine should also play that data as a drum pattern.

MIDI CONNECTIONS

MIDI-enabled hardware usually has three connections: MIDI in, MIDI out, and MIDI thru. As the name suggests, the In connection is for incoming data, the Out connection is for outgoing data, and the Thru connection sends an exact copy of any incoming MIDI data to another device. Data sent via the Thru connection isn't affected by

anything you do on that particular device, so for example
if you're playing a keyboard, anything you do won't be sent
via the Thru port.

MINIDISC

Sony's replacement for ancient tape cassettes, MiniDisc
uses a tiny recordable disc to store around an hour's worth
of music. Sound quality isn't as good as CD, but it's not
far off it.

"Finally! All your hits on one nano-disc Mr Jackson!"

MIXING

Mixing is the process of turning a recording into something that's worth listening to. The mixing engineer sets the volume of each instrument, tweaks the EQ, adds effects and generally tinkers with the various parts of a recording until it sounds good. Not to be confused with remixing, which takes elements of an existing song and creates something new and interesting – or something dull and derivative, depending on the remixer.

MP3

MP3 is a way of turning music into tiny computer files, which can then be played on portable players, burned to CDs or traded illegally over the Internet.

MP3PRO

Developed by the same people who invented MP3, mp3PRO is a new format that offers better sound quality than normal MP3s. However, at the time of writing it seems that music fans couldn't care less, and mp3PRO may well go the way of the dodo, the 8-track cartridge and **George Michael's** solo career.

THE CUT THE CRAP! GUIDE TO: **MUSIC TECHNOLOGY**

MULTIFX

Short for **Multiple Effects**, a MultiFX unit is anything that enables you to add several different effects to an instrument. MultiFX boxes are most commonly used for guitarists, and provide quick access to effects such as distortions, delays and choruses.

NAPSTER

Napster hit the headlines when the controversial file sharing service introduced a generation to the joys of free – if not exactly legal – music on the Internet. After endless lawsuits the service was finally shut down in 2002, but its legacy lives on in the form of Napster-style systems such as **Kazaa**.

NORMALISING

With digital formats such as CD, there's a limit to how loud you can make a track: go beyond it, and you get a harsh clicking noise that's painful to listen to and bad news for your speakers. Normalising is part of the mastering process, and it ensures that songs don't exceed the maximum level for CDs and other digital formats.

OGG VORBIS

An alternative to MP3, **Ogg Vorbis** isn't owned by anybody – like the **Mozilla** browser, it's the work of volunteers – and it offers sound quality that makes MP3 look rather pathetic. It's still a fairly obscure format but it has a number of advantages over MP3 competitors such as **Windows Media**, not least the fact that it doesn't contain any copy protection technology.

PLUGIN

A plugin is a software program that 'plugs in' to a bigger one. For example, you can buy reverb plugins that work with **ProTools**, compressors that work with **Acid Pro**, or digital delays that work with **Cubase**. Although most music software comes with a basic set of effects (EQ, reverb and so on), dedicated plugins generally offer better control and better sound quality.

PROTOOLS

Depending on who you talk to, **ProTools** is either the best thing that's happened to music since the electric guitar, or the worst. **DigiDesign's** software enables engineers or musicians to chop up songs, fix bits that are out of time, and add effects. Teamed up with software such as AutoTune, **ProTools** can turn a rubbish singer into an exceptional one.

See also: **AutoTune**

PUBLIC DOMAIN

All songs are copyrighted, which means that only the composer can produce copies of the work without permission (and payment). However, copyrights expire – at the moment, UK copyrights expire 70 years after the death of the author – and if they're not renewed by the author's descendants, they pass into the public domain. This means that nobody owns the song, and that you can record and release a version of it – or a song that samples it – without paying royalties to anybody.

See also: **Copyright, Royalties**

QUICKTIME

Apple's media technology is designed for music and video on the Internet, and can be used to provide downloads or to 'stream' music on the Net.

See also: **Streaming**

RAM

Short for **Random Access Memory**, RAM is a measure of computer memory. The bigger the number, the more memory you have. This is particularly important if you want to make multitrack music on a computer, because you need sufficient memory to deal with all the tracks at once. For example, a typical CD-quality stereo track takes up just over 10MB of memory, so to use ten tracks you'll need 100MB – over and above the memory used by the program itself. In practice, that means a machine with less than 256MB of RAM will find it hard to cope with multitrack music.

REALAUDIO [AKA REAL MEDIA, REALVIDEO]

Originally a technology for streaming audio on the Internet, **RealAudio** was joined by **RealVideo** and relaunched as **Real Media**. **Real Media** files can be streamed on the Net, but the developers would also like you to think of **Real Media** as an alternative to MP3.

See also: **Streaming**

RIPPING

The process of turning a song on a CD into an MP3 file on your computer is known as 'ripping'.

SAMPLER

A sampler is a bit of hardware that 'samples' sounds, enabling you to reuse those sounds in your own music. You could sample old records or your own voice, then use the sampler to edit and play back the section(s) you want. Samplers are usually used with keyboards or sequencers, for example, so that pressing a certain key 'triggers' the appropriate sample.

THE CUT THE CRAP! GUIDE TO: **MUSIC TECHNOLOGY**

SAMPLING

Sampling refers to two different things: in songs, sampling is when you 'sample' part of someone else's music – from a snare drum sound to a few bars of music – and use it in your own compositions; in computers, sampling is the way in which computers turn music into data. For example, CDs use a sampling rate of 44.1KHz, or 44,100 samples per second.

"Wicked! This will make a bangin' snare sample!"

SAMPLING RATE

The sampling rate tells you the quality of a sample: for example, CD-quality music is sampled at a rate of 44.1KHz, or 44,100 samples per second. DVDs use 96KHz sampling, or 96,000 samples per second.

Things get confusing when people talk about sampling rates for MP3 music files, because the numbers use a different format. A 160Kbps MP3 file is still sampled at 44.1KHz, but it uses compression to reduce the file size; an MP3 file encoded at 128Kbps needs 128 kilobits (16 kilobytes) of space for every second of music, while a CD-quality WAV file needs 1,411 kilobits per second.

See also: **Kbps**

SEQUENCER

Sequencers are special types of computers (or more often these days, computer programs) that are designed for making music. A sequencer enables you to program a sequence of notes, such as a bassline; once programmed, the sequencer can then control keyboards and other MIDI-enabled instruments and make them play your sequence. They're a boon for musicians who need a lot of different things to play at once, but who don't have eight pairs of arms to operate all their gear.

THE CUT THE CRAP! GUIDE TO: **MUSIC TECHNOLOGY**

SEQUENCING

Sequencing is another word with two meanings. In music making, it's the use of a sequencer to create programmed 'sequences' such as bass lines or melody parts; in record manufacturing, sequencing is the process of deciding in which order songs should appear on an album.

SOUND MODULE

A sound module is a piece of MIDI hardware or an add-on for a keyboard that contains accurate models of various musical instruments. If you connect the module to a keyboard or sequencer, you can then use those sounds – from realistic grand piano sounds to things from the darker corners of the **BBC** sound effects library.

STREAMING

A clever type of technology – used in **Windows Media**, **QuickTime** and **Real Audio** – that means you can listen to music without spending 200 years downloading a computer file. Streaming technology sends music (or video) to your computer in tiny chunks, and once you've received enough chunks you can watch the clip or listen to the song. Streaming is best suited to low-quality previews, for example so people can hear your music without first downloading MP3 files.

See also: **Windows Media, QuickTime, Real Audio**

SYNTHESISER

A synthesiser is an instrument that 'synthesises' sounds. For example, instead of lugging a church organ around with you, you could use a keyboard that synthesises the sound of an organ. These days, synthesisers are incredibly realistic and can replicate the sound of any instrument you can imagine – and some that you can't imagine without eating lots of cheese at bedtime.

TOPPING AND TAILING

Part of the mastering process, topping and tailing means getting rid of unwanted noise at the beginning and end of a track.

UNCLEARED SAMPLE

An uncleared sample is a bit of someone else's song that the artist or label hasn't got permission to use. Uncleared samples are a good way to attract the attention of heavyweight music industry lawyers.

See also: **Sampling**

WINDOWS MEDIA

Microsoft's rival to MP3 can handle audio and video files, and can be used for audio/video streaming or for downloads. Record companies love it, because it's packed with copy protection technology that can be used to prevent people making illegal copies of music files.

ZZZZZ

The noise people make if you talk about technology when you're supposed to be relaxing in the pub.

APPENDIX: USEFUL SITES

MUSICIANS' RESOURCES

Boom Selection

www.boomselection.net

Everything you ever wanted to know about the MP3
bootlegging scene.

CD Baby

www.cdbaby.net

A well-respected site that helps independent musicians
sell CDs on the Internet.

Dancetech

www.dancetech.com

One of the best resources on the Internet for dance music,
with extensive information and advice on everything from
recording to product reviews.

Drowned in Sound

www.drownedinsound.com

Excellent UK webzine that's read by many industry
insiders.

eBay

www.ebay.co.uk

This auction site is a good place to look for second-hand
recording equipment.

The Free Music Philosophy
www.ram.org/ramblings/philosophy/fmp.html
Ram Samudrala reckons that you can make money by giving your music away for free – and he might be right. Find out more on his website.

Future of Music Coalition
www.futureofmusic.org
Although it's aimed at American artists, the Future of Music Coalition is still packed with relevant information about music technology and copyright law.

Indiecentre
www.indiecentre.com
An excellent collection of advice and information for independent labels.

Indie-music.com
www.indie-music.com
Billing itself as the place 'where serious musicians surf', Indie-music.com hosts a staggering amount of useful information on every aspect of the music business.

Piedog
www.piedog.com
One of the best-known online music shops in the UK, Piedog makes it easy to find and compare different musical equipment. It's also worth checking out www.soundcontrol.co.uk, www.guitarstrings.co.uk and www.soundslive.co.uk, or any of the dozens of online gear shops.

THE CUT THE CRAP! GUIDE TO: **MUSIC TECHNOLOGY**

OneMusic

www.bbc.co.uk/radio1/onemusic

Radio 1's site for unsigned bands offers the usual 'get famous by uploading your music!' nonsense, but it's also packed with useful information from industry insiders.

Sonic State

www.sonicstate.com

News, advice, contacts and discussion forums for electronic musicians with particularly good information on home recording and synth gear.

Starpolish

www.starpolish.com

In addition to hosting the Velvet Rope discussion forum (see Music Industry Message boards) Starpolish is also a good source of advice on DIY promotion.

Tweakheadz

www.tweakheadz.com

An excellent source of how-to guides for electronic musicians, covering MIDI, sequencers, samplers and synths.

Vitaminic

www.vitaminic.co.uk

One of the best MP3 sites on the Web, Vitaminic enables you to sell MP3 music or give it away to attract new fans.

MUSIC INDUSTRY MESSAGE BOARDS

The Tip Sheet
www.tipsheet.co.uk
The A&R insider's magazine is now defunct but its message board is still useful.

The Hit Sheet
www.hitsheet.co.uk
A new rival to the **Tip Sheet** that recommends the best demos to A&R staff.

Record of the Day (formerly Clickboardroom)
www.recordoftheday.com/mb/
Another **Tipsheet** rival with an exceptionally busy industry message board.

The Velvet Rope
www.starpolish.com/velvetrope/ubbthreads/ubbthreads.php
US version of the **Tip Sheet**; interesting if you're thinking of contacting US companies.

COMPUTER MUSIC

Harmony Central
www.harmony-central.com
Extensive gear and software reviews with links to decent download sites. An essential bookmark for computer musicians.

Sonic Foundry
www.sonicfoundry.com
Music and video editing programs including *Sound Forge* and *Acid Pro*.

DigiDesign
www.digidesign.com
Manufacturer of **ProTools**, the industry standard music software program.

Steinberg
www.steinberg.de
Software includes *Cubase VST*, *WaveLab* and **Steinberg** *Mastering Edition*.

MusicMatch
www.musicmatch.com
MusicMatch Jukebox is a free MP3 player that can turn your CDs into shiny digital computer files.

Real Networks
www.real.com
Real Networks provides a range of free software that enables you to create CDs or put music on the Web with its **RealAudio** format.

Windows Media
www.windowsmedia.com
Real Networks' main rival offers similar technology and software, but promises even better sound quality for Internet music.

Propellerhead Software
www.propellerheads.se
Creators of the popular *Rebirth* and *Recycle* programs, which emulate old drum machines, sequencers and synths on your computer.

WEB DESIGN SOFTWARE

Dreamweaver
www.macromedia.com
One of the best Web design programs you can get, but at £200 it's not cheap. If you're a student, you can get cut-rate educational licenses.

GoLive
www.adobe.com
Adobe's competitor to *Dreamweaver* is particularly popular with Mac users. Pricing is similar to *Dreamweaver* and educational discounts are available.

HotMetal Pro
www.hotmetalpro.com
At around £70, **HotMetal** offers a lot of power for a very reasonable price – but it's not for Web design beginners.

Netscape Composer
www.netscape.com
If you're new to Web design or just don't fancy paying lots of money for software, the free Netscape Composer is a good starter program.

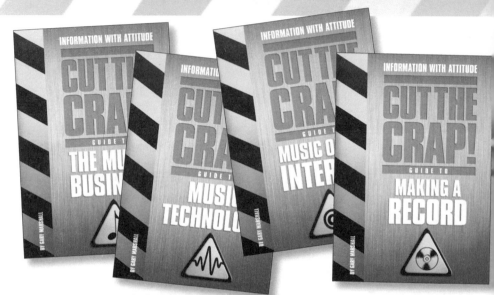